This book documents some of the change that has occurred in Sacramento's relatively short but fascinating history. To do this, we first tracked down old black-and-white photographs of prominent or interesting locations. Some of these pictures dated back 100 years or more; the most recent was made in 1961. Then, we returned to those locations to shoot new color photographs from the exact spot the original picture was made. In some instances, the original view was obscured by trees or buildings that have sprouted in the interim. In those cases, the angle of the new picture may differ slightly from the old. Though this book reaches into Sacramento's past, its purpose is not to provide a definitive history of the city. We believe you'll find the photographs published here to be interesting and, perhaps, enlightening.

Sacramento THEN & NOW

STEVE MELLON

Introduction By
Charlene Gilbert Noyes

Edited & Designed by
J. BRUCE BAUMANN
COPYRIGHTED © 1994
SCRIPPS HOWARD PUBLISHING, INC.
ALL RIGHTS RESERVED

High above Sacramento, a group of more than fifty planes fly over downtown. More than likely, the event was part of the Great Maneuvers, a military airplane exercise based at Mather Field which occurred in April 1930. The Army Air Corps participated in the three-week mock war games over the skies of northern California. Air units from bases in Texas, Michigan, Virginia, and California engaged in the largest concentration of United States military aircraft at that time.

ow the Tower Bridge instead of the M Street Bridge spans the Sacramento River at Capitol Mall. The newly built sky-scrapers as well as Sacramento's early high rises, the Cal-Western Building and the Elks Building, add height to the downtown area. The State Capitol still sits at the end of Capitol Mall and even a riverboat still is docked along the waterfront.

Sacramento THEN & NOW

Sacramento, California's capital, has experienced in its relatively short history tremendous growth and changes. An important commercial and transportation center for over 150 years, it currently is the forty-first largest city in the United States, according to 1990 census figures.

The first inhabitants of the area were the Nisenan Indians, a linguistic group of the Maidu tribe, who settled along the two major rivers, the American and to a lesser extent, the Sacramento. Once contact with European settlers occurred, the Nisenan were subjected to diseases for which they had little or no immunity. Their population diminished rapidly. Approximately seventy-five percent of the population died as the result of a malaria epidemic in 1833. The Gold Rush period led to another significant decline in the Nisenan's population. By the 1960s, only a handful of Native Americans residing in Sacramento were of Nisenan ancestry.

In 1808 Gabriel Moraga, a Spanish explorer, set out from Yerba Buena (San Francisco) to explore the vast territory which lay northeast of that settlement. Upon coming to the rivers we know today as the American and the Sacramento, he designated them the Llagas and the Jesus Maria, respectively. Further upstream, thinking that the Feather River was an arm of the Jesus Maria, he named it the Sacramento, meaning "holy sacrament" in Spanish. Although others, who followed, corrected his oversight, the name Sacramento survived, and later visitors used it for other geographical terms.

The area's most significant event occurred in 1839 when a Swiss entrepreneur, John A. Sutter, navigated up the Sacramento and American Rivers from Yerba Buena and landed on a site near 28th and B Streets. Captain Sutter, as he called himself, soon established Sutter's Fort nearby and forever changed the region. He obtained his eleven league land grant, New Helvetia, meaning New Switzerland, from the Mexican government. The 1848 discovery of gold at his Coloma sawmill, forty-five miles eastward, soon resulted in the thriving city of Sacramento.

Changes occurred rapidly. Sacramento was now a logical transportation and commercial center for wealth seeking miners and business people, hoping to take advantage of the miners' needs. John Sutter Jr., to whom the elder Sutter gave power of attorney, laid out Sacramento City in 1849 and sold lots through his agent, Peter H. Burnett, who would become California's first governor. An earlier attempt by the elder Sutter to establish a town several miles south of Sacramento called Sutterville was now destined for failure.

Besides the tremendous growth of the new city, Sacramento also had its share of disasters. A cholera epidemic in late 1850 killed over 600 individuals and sent many scurrying from the city. Early floods and fires caused citizens to rethink the manner in which they built their businesses, streets, and homes. A dispute over land escalated into the Squatters Riot in 1850 and ended with the mayor, sheriff, and city assessor being shot. The sheriff and city assessor died during the riot, and the mayor eventually died from the wounds he sustained.

The floods and fires require elaboration because of the resulting changes in the downtown area. Floods in January 1850, March 1852, and December 1852, caused Sacramentans to realize that a low-lying city built near the confluence of two rivers was destined to have such problems. The logical solution then, would be to raise the streets to a higher level. In the winter of 1861-62, when Sacramento received the most rainfall ever recorded, it became obvious that the downtown streets and buildings needed to be raised even higher. After all, Sacramento had become the permanent capital of California in 1854, and many non-Sacramentans saw the floods as a good excuse to move the capital permanently to a less troublesome location.

As if flooding were not enough, fires in 1850, 1852, and 1854 also took their toll on the fledgling city. The worst of the three blazes occurred on a windy night on November 4, 1852. By the next morning, seven-eighths of the downtown business district was destroyed. Merchants began building their structures from brick as a preventive measure.

The remainder of the nineteenth century was less tumultuous than what transpired in the first few decades of the city. The focus was now on transportation; namely the railroad. The Sacramento Valley Railroad, completed in 1856, connected Sacramento with Folsom, twenty-three miles to the east, and was California's first railroad. In 1869, the Transcontinental Railroad, completely finished, brought new residents and Easterners to Sacramento via a much easier route than earlier travelers experienced via the overland and sea routes.

The construction boom of the 1920s forever changed the skyline of Sacramento. Structures such as the Elks, Cal-Western, Southern Pacific Depot, Fruit Exchange, and Library and Courts buildings, and Memorial Auditorium soon gave Sacramento an even more recognizable skyline.

Although the Depression slowed growth, post World War II expansion saw Sacramento grow tremendously. New housing developments such as River Park sprang up and replaced farm land. Suburban shopping centers now were

common. Soon a four-year college, Sacramento State College opened its doors on land which had once been peach orchards. The automobile became an even more important transportation mode, when the last street car ceased to operate in 1947.

Downtown redevelopment in the 1950s and 1960s caused many Sacramento landmarks to be demolished. Parking lots, new civic buildings, and new businesses replaced the homes and businesses Sacramentans had known for years. M Street, between Front and Tenth Streets, was transformed into Capitol Mall; and K Street became a pedestrian and shopping mall from Third to Fourteenth Streets.

Redevelopment projects transformed Sacramento's west end area from a declining skidrow into the historic "Old Sacramento" district we know today. But not without a battle over the routing of Interstate 5. Three routes were suggested for the north-south freeway. One would pierce through the center of the historic district of "Old Sacramento;" another would travel through Yolo County instead of Sacramento; and the last suggestion was to elevate the freeway and miss the waterfront section of the historic district. The Highway Commission chose the latter plan for its final decision.

In the 1850s during its first decade as a city, Sacramento grew 102 percent in population from 6,820 to 13,785. Large growth also occurred in the teens, twenties, and thirties, when population grew from 45,000 to 106,000. Much of the growth is attributable to a major annexation of the East Sacramento, Curtis, Land, and Oak Park areas in 1912. Other annexations, such as that of the entire City of North Sacramento in 1964, further expanded Sacramento's population.

Today, Sacramento is the twenty-second fastest growing urban area in the United States. The city has a population of well over 385,000, and once again is experiencing a construction boom. New structures such as the Renaissance Tower, the Wells Fargo Building, the Hyatt Regency, the U.S. Bank Plaza, the new State Library Annex, and the State Archives Building

are changing the landscape. The city's convention center is currently undergoing expansion, as well.

Regional Transit's "light rail" trains carry Sacramento shoppers and workers to and from downtown and the suburbs. The National Basketball Association team, the Kings, made Sacramento its home in 1985 at the Arco Arena in the Natomas area of Sacramento. Thursday Night Market on the K Street Mall has brought life back into the downtown area on Thursday evenings. Now thousands of shoppers flock to enjoy food, music, entertainment, and farm fresh produce.

As you can see from the following photographs, Sacramento has changed dramatically. Many of its landmarks are only memories, stimulated by photographs such as these. Yet, in between the new high rises and freeways are hidden the rich history that makes Sacramento a very unique city.

– Charlene Gilbert Noyes

This oldest known photograph of Sacramento, a daguerreotype, taken in 1850 by George Johnson, depicts the Sacramento waterfront with its newly constructed buildings at the foot of K Street. The side-wheeler, New World, had the distinction of bringing good and bad news to Sacramento in 1850. The good news was that on September 9, 1850, Congress had admitted California into the Union as the 31st state. Unfortunately, the bad news was that one of the passengers on board was stricken with cholera. The ensuing epidemic left hundreds dead. Notice the man working on the vessel's side by the letter "N."

Today a different paddle wheeler is docked at Sacramento's waterfront. The Delta King, recently renovated as a restaurant, lounge, and floating hotel, now permanently resides along the waterfront. The Delta King and its sister ship, the Delta Queen, used to ply up and down the Sacramento River to San Francisco in the 1920s and 1930s. During World War II both transported troops from assembly camps to troop ships in San Francisco Bay and served as temporary housing and hospital ships for the troops. The Delta Queen today steams the Mississippi River as an excursion boat and hotel.

obert Frazee, a city police officer, poses with his horse and family in front of his home at 18th and F Streets. The home originally faced F Street and later was moved to face 18th Street. Frazee died in 1892, just a few years after this photograph. His white horse participated in the funeral procession carrying his master's boots backwards in the stirrups.

T he neighborhood is still residential today and apartments now occupy the site.

Designed by Sacramento architects Starks and Flanders, the California Fruit Exchange building at 10th and N Streets was completed in 1932. The attractive Spanish Colonial Revival designed building is complemented by the corner tower. From 1932 to 1966 the Exchange kept its headquarters in this building, which is directly across from the State Capitol.

Now the State of California uses the building for offices. The building is
listed on the National Register for Historic Places. The taller building
behind the Fruit Exchange is the Resources Building, owned
by the State of California.

The Central Pacific Railroad built this structure specifically as a hospital for railroad workers in 1869. Later, the building was referred to as the Southern Pacific Hospital to reflect the name change of the railroad company. This building at 13th and C Streets served as the hospital until 1901 when the hospital moved into the former Charles Crocker home in Sacramento. Railroad employees' dues helped support the administration of the hospital.

An automotive lighting and safety equipment business now occupies the site of the old hospital.

The winter of 1861-62 was Sacramento's wettest on record. The worst month, January 1862, saw 15" of rain fall in a matter of a few days, an amount almost equal to Sacramento's annual rainfall total. Needless to say, several floods occurred in the city. Afterward, to prevent future disasters, the city strengthened the existing levees and further raised the streets and buildings in the downtown area with tons of dirt and determination. The boaters in this view are at K and Front Streets, going eastward.

S acramento's business district, known as the West End, began to decline in the 1920s as cheap hotels and bars began to replace other businesses. The Redevelopment Agency of the City of Sacramento and the State of California initiated redevelopment plans for the district and saved many of its historic buildings through restoration and reconstruction. Today, Old Sacramento, bounded by Front, Second, I Streets and Capitol Mall is a registered National Historic Landmark.

Sandwiched between the Sacramento Public Library and the Californian Hotel on the 800 block of I Street, the San Fong Chong Laundry operated from 1910-1945. Businessman Michael Miller constructed the building in the mid-1890s. In later years the business served as a real estate agency office and a bail bond agency.

N ow the newly expanded Sacramento Public Library stands in place of the brick building and runs the full length of the block between 9th and 8th Streets on I Street.

Sacramentans have enjoyed shopping at Weinstock's Department Store for over a century. Weinstock's began in 1874 as David Lubin's, a general merchandise store which boasted only one final price on each piece of merchandise. Later, Lubin's half-brother, Harris Weinstock, entered into the business and the name became the Mechanics Store. With the store's success, once again the named changed, this time to Weinstock Lubin & Company. In 1924 when this store at 12th and K Streets opened, Sacramentans could shop and enjoy such luxuries as child care.

The building, modeled after a famous Parisian department store, still stands today and now houses offices on the K Street Mall. Weinstock's today has locations throughout California and the West.

The Moorish style Alhambra Theater opened in 1927 on 31st Street, which soon became Alhambra Boulevard to reflect the name of this beautiful showplace. The grounds featured fountains, urns, and extensive archways. Many Sacramentans remember fondly going to the movies at the Alhambra.

In 1972 news of the impending demolition of the Alhambra for a grocery store polarized the preservation community. Although a committee was formed to save the venerable theater, the building was still destroyed in May 1973. The only reminders of the once grand theater are the palm trees at the foot of Alhambra Boulevard and a fountain that was spared. In the background, a water tower looms over the grocery store.

Built in 1870 for entrepreneur Francis Fratt, this building at 2nd and K Streets served as his residence and office for many years. The beautiful ornamentation of the balcony railing and the embellishments over the arched windows made this one of the more architecturally significant buildings in the business district. It later served as the Alaskan Hotel, a drug store, and an employment agency.

The original structure was demolished in 1969 after transients started one too many fires in the old building. Later it was reconstructed as part of the Old Sacramento redevelopment project. Now the building functions as a restaurant and offices.

Margaret Crocker, wife of Judge Edwin Crocker, provided the funds for construction of the Bell Conservatory in 1881. Located across the street from the City Cemetery at 10th and Y Streets, its purpose was to provide flowers for gravesites of the poor. It also functioned as a greenhouse for exotic plants. The Geisrieter family later owned the property and operated a nursery and flower shop there. Their stationery boasted that the streetcar line stopped at the nursery every fifteen minutes.

M ost recently, a union hall has occupied the site. The union hall building was previously a grocery store.

M iller Park is in its early stages of development in this aerial image. Alice A. Miller bequeathed the thirty-two acres for the park to the City of Sacramento in 1942. She asked that the park be named for her brother, Frederick A. Miller, and designated the land be used for public purposes such as a park and boat harbor. The City began to develop the marina in the 1950s, and also added a baseball diamond and soccer field.

1994

Today this popular marina always has a waiting list for berth spots. Interstate 5 curves along the Sacramento River in the contemporary photograph of the park. The snow-capped Sierra Nevada Mountains in the previous image are rarely visible today through the haze.

ocated at the southwest corner of 8th and J Streets in downtown Sacramento, this building, originally built as the People's Bank, has undergone many name changes in its history. It later became a larger office for A. P. Giannini's Bank of Italy, which later became Bank of America. The bank's busiest days were Southern Pacific employees' paydays. Even more exciting was payday for Mather Air Force Base when an armed guard used to drive to the bank and pick up cash to pay the base personnel. The streets around the bank were closed while the transaction occurred each month.

T he building was razed in 1960 to make way for a Bank of California office and multi-deck garage.

The northeast corner of 5th and K Streets was in the heart of Sacramento's business district. Many different businesses appear in this image, including a dentist's and doctor's office, a restaurant, an import deli, a candy store, a clothing store, and Blumberg's Hat Works, which is featured later at another address.

Seventy years later, K Street is now a semi-covered shopping mall, Downtown Plaza, which offers many of the same shopping choices as the stores in the original image.

The owner of the Old Corner Saloon, William M. Ellsworth, stands in front of his saloon in the heart of downtown. In 1887, the year of the photograph, customers could enjoy a beer for 5 cents. The saloon later became the Arlington Saloon.

A stark contrast to the 1887 view, 6th and K Streets is now the central portion of the recently remodeled Downtown Plaza. Coincidentally, the contemporary store's name, Casual Corner, reflects partially the original store's name.

1935

Construction of the Tower Bridge, one of the city's most visible landmarks, began in July 1934. The new bridge was built to replace the old M Street Bridge. Ten thousand people attended the dedication ceremonies on December 15, 1935 and heard Governor Frank Merriam formally dedicate the bridge. The release of 1,000 homing pigeons and a parade of decorated yachts in the Sacramento River helped provide a festive mood to the event.

Sacramento Northern tracks originally stretched down the middle of the expanse with traffic lanes and sidewalks on either side. Recently, a lighting project in celebration of Sacramento's sesquicentennial in 1989 added new highlights to the bridge.

Inside Maintenance Building 251, McClellan Field personnel service B-29 bombers. The B-29 was the same model plane that dropped the atomic bomb on Hiroshima and Nagasaki, Japan.

oday Building 251 is still in use at McClellan Air Force Base. In this photograph, McClellan personnel are servicing F-111 fighter bombers. McClellan Field opened in 1939 and now that Mather Air Force Base has closed, is the only remaining active Air Force base in Sacramento County.

The Sacramento Hotel, completed in 1909, was one of Sacramento's premiere lodging establishments. The city desperately needed a topnotch hotel because of its status as the capital. The building, situated on the southeast corner of 10th and K Streets, even accommodated President William Howard Taft during his visit to Sacramento in September 1911. The Walnut Room restaurant and bar was a long-time favorite gathering spot for legislators and Sacramentans. Note the canopies on the west side of the hotel, a much needed shield against the hot Sacramento sun.

The wrecking ball demolished the old hotel in 1956 to make way for the present day Woolworth's Store, part of the K Street Mall.

A. J. Pommer's business began as a sewing machine store and later in 1890 expanded to sell both sewing machines and music related items. The famous Sherman & Clay Company later owned the store, also selling musical instruments and accessories. The building also functioned as the Arcade Bar and later served as a delicatessen.

Today a high-rise office structure which comprises part of the U.S. Bank Plaza occupies this location at 9th and J Streets.

Completed in 1889 under the direction of Bishop Patrick Manogue, the Cathedral of the Blessed Sacrament replaced the St. Rose of Lima Catholic Church, located at 7th and K Streets. The Cathedral, located at 11th and K Streets, is the city's oldest and largest church, its spire rising 216 feet and topped with a gold cross. The other church at the far right of the image is the old Evangelical Lutheran Church at 12th and K Streets.

1994

Today the Cathedral, which recently celebrated its 100th anniversary, still serves Sacramento's Catholic community. A recent restoration project has returned the church to its original beauty. Now the high rise at 1201 K Street dwarfs the Cathedral.

Taken from the I Street Bridge looking southward, the two scenes contrast Sacramento's changing commercial and transportation focus. In this 1937 scene, many boats as well as the River Lines wharf, offices, and warehouse appear on the left side just north of the Tower Bridge. The River Lines operated the Delta King and Delta Queen from this location.

S tair step buildings on the left of the contemporary picture seem to
descend to the Sacramento River. The buildings are, from left to
right, the Wells Fargo Center, the Capitol Square Building, and the
Capitol Bank Center.

S acramento's oldest suburb, Oak Park, was the home of the Silva Saloon at 3500 Sacramento Avenue. Michael Silva first acquired the neighborhood bar in 1912. Andrew Nygren originally owned the building, which he built around 1902 as a saloon. Silva operated the saloon from 1912 until Prohibition in 1920. After that, he sold soft drinks.

1994

An auto tire store, surrounded by a high security fence, now sits on the triangular lot.

The Woodlake Service Station at Del Paso Boulevard and Southgate Road, in North Sacramento, holds its own against rising flood waters, as it blends with the surrounding Tudor style homes. Del Paso is named for the Mexican land grant, Rancho Del Paso, which encompassed the North Sacramento area. The Woodlake area is still a section of North Sacramento today.

N ow the site, a used car lot,
is in the midst of an area
slated for redevelopment.

ooking west down McKinley Boulevard from San Antonio Way, the newly constructed
Theodore Judah School appears on the right of the photograph. Built in three phases begin-
ning in 1937, the first phase structure cost $50,000 to build and accommodated 200 pupils
when it opened. Noted architect Charles F. Dean designed the school to replace a previous one-
room, wooden schoolhouse. The homes on the left, also newly constructed, are typical of the
McKinley Park neighborhood of East Sacramento.

L arge shade trees now help to keep the temperature cool along McKinley Boulevard. The Theodore Judah School (hidden in the trees) is the oldest continuously operated school building in Sacramento.

c.1900

Dedicated on November 28, 1889, by the Grand Officers of the Knights of Pythias of California, the Pythian Castle at the northwest corner of 9th and I Streets served as the fraternal hall. Later, the building functioned as Howe's Normal Academy and Business College. The old castle came down in 1931 to make way for the modern, new post office.

B uilt in 1933 and designed by local architects, Starks and Flanders, the new main post office replaced the older structure at 7th and K Streets. Today, federal offices as well as a branch post office are housed in the building, located across the street from City Hall.

The Sacramento Grammar School, completed in 1873, was built upon one of the park blocks donated by John Sutter, Jr. to the City of Sacramento at 15th and 16th, I and J Streets. In June 1910, the Board of Education changed the name to the Mary J. Watson School in honor of the school's long-time principal, who had resigned earlier from the position.

The City of Sacramento demolished the school in the early 1920s to build the new Memorial Auditorium, in memory of Sacramento's World War I and Spanish-American War heroes. U. S. Senator Hiram Johnson, a Sacramento native, spoke at the dedication ceremony in February 1927 and reminisced about his childhood days attending the grammar school on the auditorium site. Over the years, the auditorium has held events ranging from graduation ceremonies to a concert by the Rolling Stones. Today the auditorium awaits renovation to meet earthquake standards and is currently closed.

Three German brewer, Philip Scheld, Henry Grau, and Frank Ruhstaller, established the Buffalo Brewery in 1889 at 21st and R Streets. This view, looking down 21st Street, shows the enormous size of the brewery, which at one time was the largest west of the Mississippi River. The market for their beer extended from Alaska to South America. The brewery's proximity to the R Street railroad tracks made it an ideal location for transporting the beer.

The Sacramento Bee acquired the property in the late 1940s and began to build its new headquarters, which were completed in 1953. The Sacramento Bee is Sacramento's oldest continuously operating newspaper.

This image, printed from a glass plate negative, depicts the only remaining building of the once prominent Sutter's Fort. After John A. Sutter arrived in the region in August 1839, he set forth to construct his fort and establish the first white settlement in the region. When Sutter moved north to his Hock Farm in Sutter County, the fort fell into disrepair. The fortress walls and structures soon crumbled and all that remained was the central building. Chickens and hogs were now the occupants of the building, where once California's pioneers had lived.

Finally, in 1891 the Native Sons and Daughters of the Golden West and the California State Legislature helped to finance the restoration and reconstruction of Sacramento's oldest historic site. Today visitors can tour the fort and have a chance to turn back time.

Located in the heart of the "Pocket" area of Sacramento where the Sacramento River bends, the Manuel Silveira ranch was typical of the many farm houses that dotted this predominately Portuguese region of Sacramento. Manuel Silveira (second from left) stands with his family in front of the farmhouse.

The Silveira home was destroyed in 1963 to make way for homes sold by Harmon Realty. The Pocket area is now a popular residential area in Sacramento and has seen a rapid change from agricultural to residential land use within the last thirty years. This ranch style home is typical of many in Sacramento and California.

This image, taken from the Senator Hotel, shows the Library and Courts Building at the far right still under construction. The trees and shrubs in Capitol Park are still relatively small. Construction of the capitol lasted from 1861 to 1874, delayed by political battles and the Civil War. The legislature first occupied the building in 1869.

The most significant change to the capitol from the original image is the addition of the east annex, which added much needed office space to the building in 1952. A major restoration project for the entire capitol, lasting six years and costing $70 million, was completed in 1982. Modeled after the nation's capitol, it still serves as the home of the largest state government in the country.

J ohn H. Bruning stands proudly in front of his new home at the northeast corner of 16th and K Streets. Bruning was part owner of the Bruning and Dooley Saloon at 607 K Street. He died in 1932 after working for many years at the post office.

A stark contrast to the beautiful home, a car rental agency now sits on the site.

This magnificent home, located at 16th and H Streets, was built in 1878 for Albert Gallatin, president of Huntington and Hopkins Hardware Company. Joseph Steffens, father of noted muckraker and author Lincoln Steffens, later purchased the home from Gallatin for his family residence.

1994

In 1903 it officially became the executive residence for California's governors. Ronald Reagan, the thirteenth governor to live in the mansion, moved out in 1967. The historic structure subsequently became part of the state parks system for all to enjoy.

Home of the Sacramento Solons, Edmonds Field was one of a series of ballparks on this site at Broadway and Riverside Boulevards. A fire in 1947 destroyed the stadium and damaged several nearby homes. This 1949 image shows the newly rebuilt stadium. A streetcar line conveniently brought Solons fans right to the park so they could enjoy the home-town team play their Pacific Coast League rivals. A mural of "Casey at the Bat" was located in the concession stand lobby.

The park was demolished in 1964 to make way for a Gemco store, a chain discount store. Later, a Target store replaced the Gemco store.

Loring Rixford, a San Francisco architect, designed the city
library building which opened in 1918. The Carnegie
Corporation, which helped build libraries throughout the
nation, partially funded construction of the library. The terra cotta
detailing on the building came from the famous Gladding, McBean
& Company of Lincoln, California, located thirty miles northeast of
Sacramento.

The library recently underwent a major renovation. The original building remains and has been integrated into the new library wings. Since its reopening, thousands of patrons have passed through the doors of the Sacramento Public Library. Directly behind the library is the U. S. Bank Plaza building.

Opened in 1897 as a thirty bed hospital, the newly built Mater Misericordiae Hospital, depicted in this scene, occupied the site of 23rd and R Streets. The Sisters of Mercy operated the hospital, referred to as the "Sisters" hospital, and soon began a nurse's training school at the site. In the 1920s, the Sisters opened a new hospital, Mercy Hospital, at 40th and J Streets to replace this smaller Sisters Hospital.

Today the Sacramento Bee recycling center sits on the 23rd and R Streets site. In the foreground, Regional Transit's light rail tracks have replaced the old railroad tracks originally used by the Sacramento Valley Railroad.

A busy downtown J Street shows both car and streetcar sharing the road. Prominent buildings are the Cal-Western Building on the left and the Elks Building on the right. The State Theater and the Masonic Temple at 12th and J Streets also appear. The double tracks of Pacific Gas & Electric's trolleys carried passengers as far as 46th Street in East Sacramento and was one of the most heavily traveled routes during the trolleys' heyday.

N|ow J Street runs as an eastbound, one-way street. The State Theater building no longer exists, but the other buildings still stand.

The original Fremont School pictured here faced the south side of N Street near 24th Street. Sarah Mildred Jones, one of Sacramento's early African-American teachers, taught at this grammar school from 1873 to 1895. In 1895 she became principal and served in that capacity until 1915.

I n 1922 a new brick Fremont School opened on the site of the wooden structure. As a result of California's earthquake standards, the building closed as an elementary school in 1976 and has since reopened as an adult education school.

Although usually associated with Central Pacific Railroad founder and California governor Leland Stanford, the Stanford home on N Street between 8th and 9th Streets was originally built in the 1850s for Shelton Fogus. Stanford acquired the home in 1861 and ten years later had the home extensively remodeled. In 1872 the Stanfords held one of Sacramento's most lavish parties to celebrate its completion. Famous photographer Eadward Muybridge snapped this photograph for Leland Stanford in 1872.

Today the Stanford home is a historical site in California's State Parks Department. Prior to that time, it had served as the Stanford Children's Home, through a gift from Mrs. Leland Stanford to the Catholic Church.

c.1922

This aerial photograph graphically illustrates the changes which have occurred in the northwestern part of Sacramento. Centrally located in the image is the Southern Pacific rail yard. The old depot, just off the I Street bridge, was still in use at this time, but over on I Street work is under way on the new depot as evidenced by the pile driver. The City of North Sacramento is at the top middle of the photograph. Just above the Southern Pacific yards, smoke from the chimney of the city incinerator, located at North B Street, is visible.

Today the Southern Pacific rail yard awaits redevelopment to transform it into a business and transportation center. Interstate 5 slices its way along the Sacramento River past the I Street Bridge, the same bridge as in the original picture.

Located at the northeast corner of 10th and E Streets in Alkali Flat, J. L. Dunphy Groceries has remained in the Dunphy family since the building's construction in 1868. Customers used to have charge accounts payable at month's end. Home deliveries were common with the groceries carried in collapsible boxes, which the delivery man carried back to the store. Customers were treated to personalized requests. If you needed two bunches of onions, a tomato, and ten potatoes to make soup, the groceries would be on the doorstep later that day.

The grocery store has changed little in appearance from the original photograph over seventy years ago. Dunphy's is the oldest continuously family-operated grocery store in Sacramento.

The McKinley Primary School, located at 7th and G Streets, was originally named Union School. During the 1930s, the building became headquarters for the Civilian Conservation Corps and in 1938 was demolished. The streetcar tracks in the foreground led east toward McKinley Park. Westward trains turned south on 7th Street and then eastward on T Street to 28th Street, the end of the line.

Today, the Sacramento County Sheriff's Department makes its headquarters on the old school site and is conveniently located near other county offices.

An important building in Sacramento since 1913, the Libby McNeill & Libby Fruit and Vegetable Cannery at 34th Street and Stockton Boulevard employed thousands of workers during its heyday. The cannery served as distribution center for five other Libby McNeill & Libby canneries in California. The complex contained nine brick buildings, all located near the railroad tracks, a great convenience for shipping.

Today the buildings have been thoughtfully redesigned into offices.

This grand depot, completed in 1879 by the Central Pacific Railroad, was located at the east end of the I Street Bridge just north of 2nd Street. Trains ran through the middle of the cavernous building, stopping inside to allow passengers to board and disembark. When first built, the depot was on the edge of Sutter Lake, also known as China Slough. Gradually, the lake was filled in so that by 1906 nothing remained.

In the mid-1920s construction began on the new Southern Pacific depot on I Street, and in 1926 the grand old depot was demolished. Now Interstate 5 rises over the area where the old depot once stood.

Blumberg's Hat Works, originally located on K Street, moved to its present location at 1723 J Street in the early 1920s. Several people resided in the home at the back of the business. Hats of all shapes and sizes could be cleaned and reshaped here.

Although remodeled, certain aspects of the original structure are apparent in the contemporary photograph. The building now operates as an art gallery.

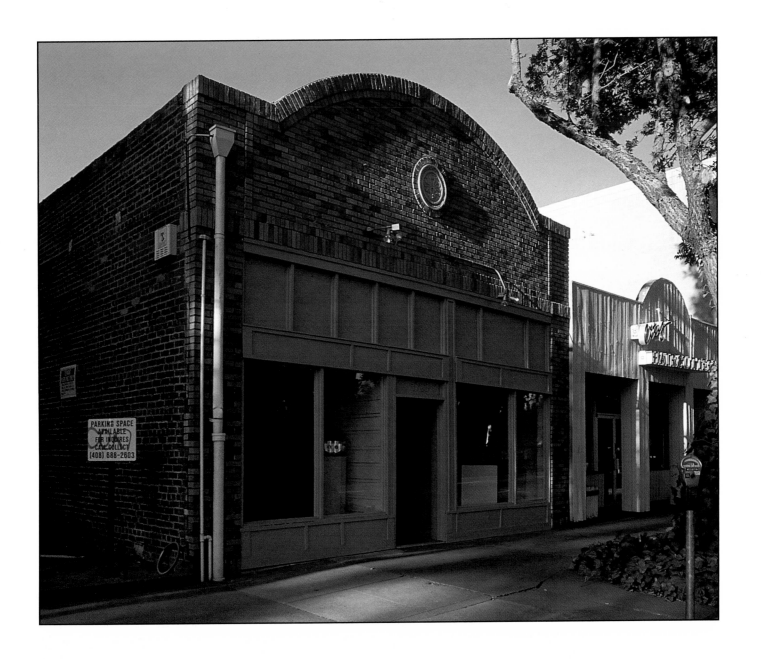

c.1953

For years Sacramentans enjoyed attending movies at the Senator Theater, located at 912 K Street. The theater opened on September 29, 1924, with a gala celebration attended by such movie stars as Corrine Griffith, Lew Cody, Eugene O'Brien, Claire Windsor, and Aileen Pringle. The theater had a grand lobby and a bridge across the alley took movie goers to the theater portion on L Street. The second floor of the K Street entrance had a ballroom.

T oday the Association of California Water Agencies owns the old theater, which now is used as office space. The L Street theater portion no longer exists.

This westward view from the capitol shows the many residences that used to line 10th Street. The homes were removed to make way for construction of State Office Building Number One in the 1920s. On the left, an unpaved M Street stretches westward toward the Sacramento River. Midpoint in the image, the Baptist Church is now the site of the Sutter Club on 9th Street.

Now the Jesse M. Unruh State Office Building occupies the area where houses once stood. The building was recently renamed for the former State Treasurer and Speaker of the Assembly from its original name of State Office Building Number One. M Street is now Capitol Mall, a mixture of federal, state, and private office buildings. The new Wells Fargo Center is barely discernible on the left, while the ubiquitous Renaissance Tower pierces the skyline on the right.

L ocated in Reclamation District 1,000, this home was typical of the style built in the Natomas area. The Natomas Company, a Folsom-based, international conglomerat which did everything from gold dredging to road building, reclaimed the land by clearing trees and brush and strengthening and building the levee system. The company then sold the land to farmers, who were eager to plant crops in the rich, alluvial soil.

Today, the Natomas area of Sacramento has become mostly a residential and commercial area. A few pockets of open land, like this one, still remain.

Sacramento's third county courthouse, designed by Rudolph Herold, was built from 1910 through 1913. From 1850 to 1970, the site at 7th and I Streets functioned solely as the courthouse, albeit in three different buildings. In October 1925 a bomb exploded in the building, shattered windows, and blew out the back door. The perpetrators were never caught.

Many Sacramentans remember fondly the beautifully designed courthouse with its cornice figures. Herold had also designed the county jail on the same block and City Hall, just down the street. The courthouse was demolished in 1970 after a new one opened at another site. The old courthouse site served as a parking lot until recently when the county constructed its new main jail facility there.

Horses stand ready in this turn-of-the-century photograph of Engine Company Number Three, located on 21st Street between L and M Streets. Company Number Three organized in 1888 and moved into its new home, pictured here in 1893. It was the oldest original operating fire station in Sacramento until decommissioned in the 1980s.

R ecently refurbished, the structure now houses a coffee house and business offices, where horses used to race from the firehouse doors.

=== *c.1950* ===

Peach orchards once grew where the California State University, Sacramento (CSUS) campus now resides. This image, taken northward and high above Folsom Boulevard, shows the Horst Ranch and hop fields to the right of the American River, where Campus Commons, a residential subdivision, is today. Homes in East Sacramento and River Park are visible at the top of the view.

Today, CSUS has over 25,000 students. On the far left of the view is Hornet Field, home to many CSUS sports events as well as the Sacramento Gold Miners, a football team in the Canadian Football League. The CSUS library is the prominent building in the center of the photograph.

c.1875

Looking southward down 2nd Street between J and K Streets, Sacramento's business district was well established by the time this image was taken. Several hotels are in this block. From foreground to background the structures on the right are the B. F. Hastings Building, the Arcade Hotel, the Adams Express Building, the Orleans Hotel, the Union Hotel, and the Bank Exchange Building.

Today 2nd Street is in the heart of Old Sacramento. Three of the buildings, the B. F. Hastings, the Adams Express, and the Bank Exchange are original. The other structures have been reconstructed, with the exception of the Orleans Hotel, which is now a vacant lot.

c.1920

Taken from the north side of the capitol dome, the image shows from left to right the William Land Hotel, the Sacramento Hotel, City Hall, the Hippodrome Theater, and the Cathedral of the Blessed Sacrament.   Some of the homes which once lined L Street can be seen through the trees.

O nly one building, the Cathedral, appears in both images. In the modern scene, the L Street homes are now replaced with an office building-parking structure complex. The Renaissance Tower on the left and the Union Bank Plaza on the right are the two tallest buildings in the picture. The Cal-Western Building in the middle obscures the view of City Hall.

Most of Sacramento's oldest residential homes are located in the Alkali Flat neighborhood, such as this building, at 925 G Street. Built in 1869 by Charles Cate, a brick maker and mason, the home was first occupied by Albert A. Van Voorhies, owner of A. A. Van Voorhies & Company, a saddlery making business.

T he home today houses a law office and is centrally located near government offices.

c.1895

Daly Brothers Groceries seemed far away from downtown in Oak Park. The store originally carried an address of 3401 Magnolia Street. In 1916 the City Commission changed hundreds of Sacramento's street names, and the new address for the store became 3401 2nd Avenue.

The old grocery store still stands today in Oak Park and is now a bicycle shop.

The third Sacramento Bee Building, shown here at 911 7th Street, was built in 1901. The Bee started in 1857 with James McClatchy as one of the reporters. McClatchy soon assumed one of the editorship roles, and the McClatchy family has been associated with the paper ever since. The Seventh Street building used to post the day's headlines on the front window, as pictured in this photograph.

The Bee moved into its new headquarters in 1953, and the 7th Street building was destroyed several years later. One of the original medieval printer embellishments and the arched entrance from this building are now displayed at the Sacramento Museum of History, Science & Technology. Today the site contains a parking lot and bank building.

Panoramas illustrate best Sacramento's changing skyline. Taken once again from the capitol, on the left the picture looks westward down Capitol Mall where State Office Building Number One and the Sutter Club are clearly visible to the right of the circular driveway. Over on L Street, the building with the three arches, located just behind the state building, is part of the Senator Theater. Farther to the right, the Cal-Western Building, the Cathedral of the Blessed Sacrament, and the Medical-Dental Building appear.

The blending of the old and new is clearly evident in this contemporary photograph in which one can see two of the city's tallest buildings, the Renaissance Tower on the left and the U. S. Bank Plaza on the right.

The 400 block of N Street pictured here was in the heart of Sacramento's Japanese neighborhood. These homes were all vacant the day Eugene Hepting took this photograph, May 16, 1942, as the Japanese-Americans were on their way to relocation camps. The families registered at Memorial Auditorium and a few days later they assembled at Camp Walerga near McClellan Field to await transfer to Tule Lake Relocation Center in Siskiyou County. In December 1944 the War Department rescinded its relocation order, and the families were able to return to what little of their property they had left. During their absence, many of these American citizens lost their homes, personal property, and jobs.

Today the newly built Wells Fargo
Center towers above N Street at
this same location.

Looking eastward on K Street from 7th Street, the most prominent building in this image is the U. S. Post Office building, erected in 1893. Its reddish sandstone color made it stand out from other more mundane buildings. The post office replaced the St. Rose of Lima church which stood at the 7th and K site until the Cathedral of the Blessed Sacrament was completed. During the Depression, the post office served as headquarters for Franklin D. Roosevelt's Works Progress Administration. By this time a new post office at 9th and I Streets had replaced this structure as the main post office.

Today, the St. Rose of Lima Park on the K Street Mall is at the site of the post office. On Thursday evenings, the Thursday Night Market brings thousands of people to the K Street Mall to enjoy foods, fresh produce, and entertainment. In winter, an outside ice skating rink sits where the church and post office once stood.

nother aerial photograph shows an ever-changing Sacramento landscape. Multi-story office buildings have replaced many of the small buildings and residences that once crowded downtown. Only a few recognizable landmarks carry over to the contemporary image. Docked just south of the Tower Bridge is either the Delta King or Delta Queen.

Today the Delta King is permanently docked just to the north of the Tower Bridge. Landmarks such as the capitol, Tower Bridge, the Crocker Art Museum, and the Library and Courts Building are featured in both images.

The east side of Capitol Park seems dwarfed in comparison to today's greenery. The park, bounded by L and N, 10th and 15th Streets, has been a long time favorite destination for Sacramentans to enjoy its lush grounds. The park contains well over 400 types of trees and plants. Near the corner of 15th and N Streets once stood the Agricultural Pavilion for the State Fair. After the new State Fair grounds on Stockton Boulevard were finished, the old pavilion was torn down.

T oday with its mature trees and shrubs, Capitol Park is a popular place to escape Sacramento's hot summer days.

S teve Mellon is a freelance photojournalist based in Pittsburgh, PA. His work appears in several national magazines and newspapers. In 1991, while working as a photographer for The Pittsburgh Press, he was named runner-up Newspaper Photographer of the Year by the National Press Photographers Association. He is an Indiana native and 1981 graduate of Eastern Kentucky University.

C harlene Gilbert Noyes received her B. A. and M. A. in History from San Jose State University in 1982 and 1984, respectively. She has been archivist at the Sacramento Archives and Museum Collection Center since 1988 and worked previously as an archivist at the California State Archives.

Captions for the photographs were researched and written by Steve Mellon and Charlene Gilbert Noyes.

Acknowledgements

This book was made possible through the assistance of the following people:

James Henley, director, Sacramento History and Science Division; Charlie Duncan, curator, Eleanor McClatchy Collection, Sacramento Archives and Museum Collection Center; Nikki Pahl, photographer; at the Sacramento Public Library, director Richard M. Killian, special collections librarian Ruth Ellis, and Suzanne Lehner, Library Assistant for Special Collections; Tom Thompson, supervisor of building trades for the State of California; helicopter pilot Jens Vilman Pederson; Kevin Bunker, of the California State Railroad Museum; Tom Gray of the Discovery Museum; Chris Seabury and Jack Hockanson of McClellan Air Force Base; long-time city residents Paul Shimada and Lawrence Perry. Sarah Logue, student intern, Sacramento Archives and Museum Collection Center.

Also...
Bill Skelton of California State University at Sacramento; Jeff Jones of Sutter's Fort State Historic Park; David West, U.S. General Services Administration; Ron Giarmona, supervisor at Old Sacramento Waterfront; Dennis Mueller of Bank of America; Verland W. Thom of Thoms Cyclery; Reynaldo Garza, capitol building maintenance worker; Wendy Hawksworth at the Governor's Mansion; and Archibald M. Mull III, Sacramento attorney. Dolores Greenslate of the Portuguese Historical Society; Don Silva, Sacramento native.

PICTURE CREDITS:

Sacramento Archives and Museum Collection Center:
Pages: 10, 12, 16, 20, 22,24, 26, 28, 30, 32, 34, 36, 42, 46, 50, 58, 62, 64, 66, 68, 74, 76, 78, 80, 84, 86, 88, 90, 92, 94, 98, 100, 102, 104, 108, 110, 112, 114, 116, 118, 120, 122,126
Special Collections of the Sacramento Public Library:
Pages: 4, 14, 18, 38, 44, 48, 52,54, 96
California State Library:
Pages: 56, 60, 70, 72, 82, 124
California State Archives:
Page: 106
McClellan Air Force Base:
Page: 40

ADDITIONAL COPIES OF THIS BOOK:

May be purchased through Sacramento Cable Television, 4350 Pell Drive, Sacramento, CA. 95838, or for additional information, call 916-927-2225.

Discounts available for bulk orders.